AF435149

contraescrita

Free Poets

the girl in black lace

eleanor bramble

contra escrithiza

the girl in black lace

the girl in black lace

eleanor bramble

co-authored by: philipe pharo

with the edition of:
Filipe Faro da Costa

Contra Escrita
Edições
2024

Author/Autora: Eleanor Bramble (pseud.)
Co-autoria: Philipe Pharo
Editor: Filipe Faro da Costa
Title/Título: The Girl In Black Lace
Collection/Coleção: Free Poets/Poetas Livres
Volume: Two/Dois
Revision/Revisão: 30th October 2024
Cover Ilustration/Ilustração de Capa: ContraatircsE
Design de Capa e Interior: ContraatircsE
Production/Produção: ContraatircsE
1st Edition/ 1ª Edição - 5th November 2024
Place of Publication/Local de Publicação:
Portugal(Arcos de Valdevez)
Legal Deposit/Depósito Legal: 538463/24
ISBN: 978-989-35418-9-0

Contact for retail orders/Contacto para encomendas a
retalho:
ContraatircsE@gmail.com

table of contents

dedication

to the girls who always knew how to value my art
— they know what i'm talking about — and to the
sweet people who made me write this madness

eleanor

acknowledgments

to my mother and father who allowed me
to commit this book

                                eleanor

preamble

it's a wonder how poetry can set someone free, the freedom of the inner self is, at the very least, the ultimate freedom of a human being, and poetry is a magnificent conveyance to allow it to come out from the deepest of our soul's bowels, at times by exposing the fears and worries of our mind and the feelings that sprout either from our heart or our dreams, other times by creating a fiercely imaginary world where we allow ourselves to pull through the other side of a locked door in our mind so to endure our fantasies, our creations, the wonder of ourselves.

eleanor bramble came to my office one day, accompanied by a friend of hers, saying she wanted to publish a poetry book; in fact, she had a different name, or should i say names, it's not likely important, what's in a name after all? she was completely assured of her goals and seeking out for the better way to achieve it. truth is she trusted me almost immediately, which was an honor, and after a prelude about writing and the strange ways we find in poetry to do it, she shared me her poetry. i must say that at first i wasn't absolutely secure about it, eleanor bramble is a young girl and the publication of her book depended on her parents in all ways, but her perseverance and mind set, along with her writing, left me cornered, also considering i've been recently translating feminist authors and by so reading women's literature, which was sort of a fortunate coincidence, i felt to be understanding the ways she expressed in her writing - go figure if a man can ever completely understand it - but as i deepened my reading of her texts it reminded me those of charlotte perkins gilman and virginia woolf, though surely with the touch of the natural naïveness of the adolescent she is, it felt profoundly feminine and was much well written with a visible knowledge of the english language that convinced me to publish the book, as long as she – and her parents - agreed to terms and to work it up with me to allow it to refrain its prosed writing style and enable it to thrive more poetically and creatively, polishing it in its form, in its words. so we did, i think, either way i'm proud of what it became and the joint work we have put into it.

might the reader disagree with some of the choices made by both of us, in the co-authoring and edition of the book, you are to know that the text arrived for disclosure mostly written in lowercase, what promptly made clear to me that eleanor bramble knew her ways into writing for publication, even though she maintained the personal pronoun "i" in uppercase, which quite hurt my sight and hurried me to change it to lowercase as the likes of e.e. cummings and rupi kaur that supported my arguments, and so all came to lowercase. also to be referred is the alternate use of the personal pronoun "you" and the modern informal use of "u" instead, which gives the text a modern and youthful trait and approach of an author that recurrently speaks directly to the reader.

i'm to say "the girl in black lace" is a work of poetry cogitated in the deepest core of the author. inherently sprouted out of her adolescence, eleanor bramble reveals us her concealed poetry from behind a plain laced flabellum. in a prosed style, but endowed with a sublime and subliminal poetry, the author sets free her verses and thoughts with a gentle and singular delicacy, expressing the contradictions and quarrels of adolescence through a charming sound, an intimate feminine and modern reflection in quest of the assertion of her desires and dreams, with a rebel and shiny touch of poetic fiction. enjoy!

philipe pharo

epigraph

POETRY

I, too, dislike it: there are things that are important beyond
*   all this fiddle.*
*   Reading it, however, with a perfect contempt for it, one*
*   discovers in*
* it after all, a place for the genuine.*
*   Hands that can grasp, eyes*
*   that can dilate, hair that can rise*
*   if it must, these things are important not because a*

high-sounding interpretation can be put upon them but because
*   they are*
* useful. When they become so derivative as to become*
*   unintelligible,*
* the same thing may be said for all of us, that we*
*   do not admire what*
*   we cannot understand: the bat*
*   holding on upside down or in quest of something to*

eat, elephants pushing, a wild horse taking a roll, a tireless
*   wolf under*
* a tree, the immovable critic twitching his skin like a horse*
*   that feels a flea, the base-*
* ball fan, the statistician—*
*   nor is it valid*
*   to discriminate against "business documents and*

school-books"; all these phenomena are important. One must make
   a distinction
however: when dragged into prominence by half poets, the
   result is not poetry,
nor till the poets among us can be
   "literalists of
   the imagination"—above
      insolence and triviality and can present

for inspection, "imaginary gardens with real toads in them,"
   shall we have
it. In the meantime, if you demand on the one hand,
the raw material of poetry in
   all its rawness and
   that which is on the other hand
      genuine, you are interested in poetry.

introduction

the poetry you'll find here doesn't seek answers. it is, above all, an invitation to reflect, a pause in the world's chaos to feel what makes us human - fragile, intense, and deeply connected to the invisible forces we sense but cannot see. open these pages as you'd open a window to your inner self. this book is a whisper from the soul. each poem within these pages is born from the depths of a heart that has been both lost and found in the tides of life.

life... isn't it sweet? i mean, it's full of madness and sadness, rage and divinity. what you choose for your freedom will decide whether your soul finds paradise. these are not just handwritten verses, they are verses written with tears and laughter, a tragic story of love and many losses, but it's still an experience, a story to tell the unknown world.

if you're trapped in your own dark fantasies, perhaps these words may offer a glimmer of light.

eleanor

5

the girl in black lace

1

pain

eleanor bramble

the girl in black lace

it was a summer day
like any other
i was listening to lana's song - cruel world -
while writing a book i'm working on

i think it's my favorite song
on the ultraviolence album
          why?
because the way her voice changes at 1:18
to something more intense and true
          understands my feelings
(that's how the idea came to me)

i'm not giving up on this one
my friends know i can never finish anything
          but this book is about how i died
i'm going to finish it

you will see
my art will be recognized
          and so will the people in it
from those who saved me to those who hurt me
i'm not gonna play the victim 'cause
i've made mistakes too
          and lots of them
(i'm sorry)

your blue eyes and blonde hair
looked like the sky with the sun to wear

burned poems

my family asks me why i write
why i close myself off
i write 'cause it helps me
when no one else does
i close myself off because i like to be alone
with my melody
(melody, not thoughts, don't get confused)

the other day i was watching a movie
where one of the main characters read the most
painful verse
yes, lisa
my eyes were also magnetic
            now they are empty

i saw my world lose its color and
the person who stole it from me never came back

before i counted the days to make sure i'd die old
(i've lost count)
i don't know when that will happen
but it won't take long
            i'm tired
happy memories should make me smile
not to write bloodstained verses

what hasn´t killed me
made me experience paradise behind the curtain
(it was horrible, it was terrible)
they took me there so i couldn't escape
i'm not afraid of the dark
but when everything goes dark and i go to the
memories lane
                everything scares me
it's always in those moments that i discover
that i'm alone
with no one to get me out of here
with no one to save me

there's a ryan's song
that a girl can't stop singing
his voice cracks as he sings
i love you enough to let u go
she didn't feel the same way and u gave her
everything

diana
you were just trying to prove that u loved her
                it wasn't your fault
please don't deceive yourself
u are talented, your poems are lived myths
(i feel them on my skin)

i still remember the one you wrote
                a while back
"they are just places (...) but for me they
will be eternal memories"
i admire your strength

15

how u're not afraid to write
what u really feel
how u are not afraid
to hide anything in poetry

i think: if i were a little like ya
i wouldn't be fighting not to be forgotten
but i can't risk telling everything
          u see
there are nightmares that are told as dreams

i'm gonna die
and i know i'm too young to think about it
but it's irresistible when all i can think
about right now is
how to end this war inside me
i will die
but my pain will forever remain in my art
my dreams, my killers, my inspiration
          forever in my burned poems
(i burned them)

"dying by your side enchants me
then i would reincarnate with u
in all other lives"
                         words from a friend

stolen happiness

in a room where gratitude is greater
          than happiness
happiness never gets in the way
i like to see other people happy
to steal genuine smiles from their
natural beauty
but his happiness...
his happiness kills me slowly

we tend to say
"what matters is that he's happy"
but what about you? are you happy?
because i bet your words are not the same
as the ones you say when
you're alone in your room
          before bed
when your mind pushes all problems away
and focuses only on the person
(the divinity left behind)

understand that
the voice says something completely different
from the look
intentions may come out innocent
from the throat
but malicious in the vast dark brown
in the deepest ocean
in the clarity of the trees
clinging to the earth so
                    as
                      not
                        to
                          fall

us girls burn before we reach heaven
and all because of something
that made us feel electric
(somebody)
we feel that touch, that heat
our imagination tortures us
with memories and sensations
the heat rises to our heads
burns us alive

we have a diamond body
beautiful and strong
it can withstand any blow
now, our heart
            we have a weak heart
and no matter how much
we want to strengthen it
the monsters won't let us
            they live inside us
and there's no way to defeat them

they are emotions... feelings
they are so strong that sometimes we give up
before we even start the fight
that's how love at first sight comes about
it's magical
butterflies are also magical
            before they fly
                out
                    of
                        our
                            throats

honestly, i don't believe in real eyes
there have been many that have fooled me
and his, oh, his eyes
damn dark eyes that made me believe
he wanted me body and soul
maybe the problem isn't in the pupils
but in me
maybe i can't read the eyes

i

can't

even

read

my

old

poetry

i have fun with tears

angels carrying flowers

you call me selfish and deluded
as if i really am
            but i'm not
i know i'm hard to get to know
but please do make an effort

i don't know how to describe myself
so i always take
people's ideas about me seriously
            i don't know
and i don't even want to describe myself
i feel like i know myself well enough
to understand the evil that lies
            behind me
but what i know about myself
i don't want to tell or show to others
because i'm afraid...
i'm afraid that someone
will take advantage of my weakness
to corner me again

anciently, anyone who would risk
a different view of the world was killed
now it's exactly the same thing
except that some people die but keep walking
have you ever thought that maybe the girl you
saw on the street is
already dead?
            she is just waiting

you don't need to have your soul stolen
to be officially dead
just have your mind ruined
and you're already destroyed
remember flowers, once a petal is plucked
it ceases to be beautiful and complete
one word and it's over
words are blades that cut our skin
without being seen
                (spilled blood doesn't ensure
                    a person's well-being)

sometimes the cure is to wait
sometimes there is no cure
and all we have left
            is to fight our own mind
it's crazy how death can be called salvation
but isn't that why
there are suicides and attempts?

she drinks vodka, he cuts himself
and i...
well, never mind

flowers are after death apologies

young and regretful

my heart was beating
my lungs were oxygenating my blood
but i wasn't alive

i was stuck in the reality i created
when nothing was going through my head
other than a good future
fifteen years of trying to live the perfect
healthy life my family wanted
i made myself believe
it was exactly what i wanted
            but it wasn't

i have a dream
or so it seemed
i was wrong when i said
i wanted to be a psychologist
i just wanted everyone to think
i was on the path to success
            i wanna be an american star
                a beautiful poetess
i wanna get out of this house
(i will be willing to face any adult problem)

          i just want to

            get out
               of
              here

father, mother
u can rest assured
i want u to know that i wasn't influenced
          i just found myself
i don't think i've ever felt so alive
since i did it

    i drank

   i laughed

    i danced

i was really happy
i know that u don't have an easy life
and that u say things without thinking
but you have no idea
how much that stops me from doing
the things i want the most

i tried so hard to follow the path
to perfection
but what for? we're all gonna die
          young and regretful
regretful because we put off until tomorrow
what we could have done today and young
because we'll never forget
what made us feel alive

the night i went out with my people
i jumped into the river with my clothes on
raised the star spangled banner
up in the air
looked up at the stars and for the first time
i saw them shining not burning
                that was me
the girl who wants to laugh
and not feel regret the next morning
the girl who wants to write
until the world knows her name

the girl who lived part of her adolescence
trapped in a false reality
it was me...
it was always me and i never knew

i had to lose everything i loved
and hated to feel that shiver
on my skin

i believe people will call me crazy
and maybe i am
but they can't call a free girl insane
can they?

i looked for myself in everyone
for a home
                for security
                                for trust
and i believe i found it
my best friend's family is like a family to me
and i love being with them
they have no shame, they just go

i think i fit into the reality
which my family finds scary
i admit i felt a little scared
when i first walked in
but there's no reason to be scared
when the only thing it makes me do
is smile

i've always been an introverted girl
(the shadow of my friends)
i'm the moon and my best friend is the sun
she makes me shine at night
sometimes a lot, sometimes a little
she's the reason the boys i love leave me
she's the light at the center of the darkness
where everyone tries to look
for it to illuminate
their vast darkening night sky

i'd be lying if i said i didn't want
            someone to love
i do
i wanna find a boy, i wanna love him
and dedicate him all my poetry
i wanna make him mine
            i don't want the attention
              my friends get
i just want to be loved, i want to be the one
i want someone who looks at my friend
and still wants me
(someone who whispers my name instead of hers)
i just wanna say - i love u -
in a true and pure way

now i have nothing to wish for
just freedom
i don't want fame
i just want people to appreciate my poems
they were very hard to write
each word was a tear
          each verse was a knife

i bled on the paper, i burned my eyes
          i killed myself:
she was too weak, afraid of being influenced
by her friends
when she was being influenced
by her own family
she was trapped, i freed her
that girl disappeared
now she lives on lane bel angels
        (the path that beautiful angels
            take to seek a new soul)

i was born to create, to discover
i believe in myself, i need to
          i can do it
              even though i know i can't

the day is unique, life is divine
if you have the opportunity today
            take it

lana once asked me:
"who are you?"
i'm the girl who wants to live
there is no point in wanting to summon death
when u are truly
alive and happy

fuck the past, it doesn't need u
the future awaits ya
think about the life u will wanna live
when u're finally free
and then tell me about your experience
tell me how good it is to be yourself
without anyone to blind u

there are memories that will haunt me forever
it's true
but everything in my mind disappears
when i'm home
and i don't mean home
i mean the outside
the street

i'm wild and i'll keep on being it
until the day i die
i'll keep being fucking crazy
until i feel like i've reached the end
and u?
will u remain trapped in this dark reality
or will u free yourself?

"wait not for tomorrow
          it might never come"

ph$_2$

american dream

they don't understand me
i really wanna go to america
i want to be american
(live the american dream)

ever since i was little
bursted within me this passion for los angeles
for art itself, however... as i said before
i never finish anything
no book, no art
but at the same time
i struggle for the world to know my name
my ideas, my story, my dreams
i want my people to know
that they're not alone

sometimes
when we have a fixed goal for a long time
it can mean that we aim to where our future
really fits

i know where i want to go
who i want to be
(have no doubts)
i wanna be a poetess
want my poems to be the tips
the readers need to free themselves
          i have the talent
u know?
i can turn mortal pain into beautiful words
they may not rhyme, but
          rhyme doesn't make poems poetry
feelings do

some told me to give up
but why?
i love writing
i was born to describe darkness as paradise
          i was born for this

do whatever u want with my art
destroy it, burn it
whatev u do
u shall not forget
years dreaming of finishing a book
and let the world to know
it was so hard
i hated my poems
          i wanted to be perfect
i didn't want to fail
at what i was really good at
i wanted to write
but no matter how hard i tried
no words would fit perfectly

u see

i was a perfectionist girl
leonor was... now me?
i don't care if my poems aren't perfect
deep down i know
my inspiration to write them
          wasn't perfect
and what she put me through
wasn't in any way pretty
often, the stories behind the scars are scary
the stories behind the poems
are equally painful
(every beauty had its tragedy, didn't it?)

i can say that... well
i don't know how i'm still writing this book
but i am
fuck, i really am

34

life can be sweet
they just need to add less salt to it

m n' s

in the spirit of madness n' sadness
i'm a soul that seeks no evil
struggle to find joy and peace
in a world of war and loss

they say i'm nothing without my poetry
and it's true
butterflies are only beautiful
                with   their   wings
(did u catch it?)
they also say i write sick things
they can't understand
my art is what makes me sweet

nothing will change me now
the war inside my mind has already begun
and i'm losing against my own thoughts

art is disappearing and that explains a lot
        love is the prologue of art
that's why i can't find anyone who stays
i think i'll be writing
'till i find someone like me
he doesn't have to be perfect
i can make him divine on my own
          i just want him to like rock
              and love me like crazy
to propose to me after three days like tommy
ya know, lee
to kill for me and not kill me
he will have no idea
but i will immortalize him in my art
(just like diana said)

---

in the spirit of madness n' sadness
i will always be in the midst of them
being consumed by madness at night
and sadness by day
don't ask me what will happen
when everything falls apart
'cause if it does... i will fall apart too

i think the hardest of days was when
i fell sick by thinking she was
giving up on me
u see
i didn't need anyone to destroy me that day

i destroyed

m
y   s
 e
l   f

what's the point of a heart
without the courage to love?

hell's angels

isn't it sweet to think
we're surrounded by flames?
that we're slowly burning?
          i think it is

if hell here is down there
then it means that for the angels up there
hell is down here
(does it makes sense?)
we are all living in hell

          we are all sinners
we ask for forgiveness when we need answers
we are not idiots, much less are we monsters

sometimes humans are the same as butterflies
we have the right to dream and achieve goals
i may not know your name
but i know u
          i know you're a dreamer
and i know what you're looking for
(i hope u find it soon)

understand
your talent is what will make you successful
don't u dare saying u're no good at anything
u are, u just don't know what
yet...
worry about finding yourself first
'cause without knowing who u are
u won't know your talent either

sometimes when people tell me
they want to get to know me better
i think back and wonder why
i don't know who i truly am
who does?
i don't have details enough
to describe my personality
(it blends as the chameleon's skin)

that's why betrayal surprises me
i only know the vein that the person
wants me to know
never the whole venous system
          knowing myself as i do now
no matter how bad the person is
i'd tell myself - u deserve her -

we are angels in hell...
in the flames that our mind created
they don't exist
(they never did)
it is all in our heads
like the monster under our bed

it never existed
          it was always inside of us
we are the person we are afraid to become
she's beautiful
(i assure u)
u don't need to be afraid of her
she will only set u free
(do u feel free?)

my thoughts are the bullets in my gun
(heavy and dangerous thoughts can kill anyone)
be careful who u choose to lose to
            life is a game of wins and losses
know your name, know your talent
know who you are

2

deception

bad mouth

why did u stop?
your love was almost enough
to make me love myself
all u had to do was to keep deceiving me

my heart broke hearing the words u said
            behind my back
my mind wandered down memory lane
and questioned myself
if everything we went through was true love
or hidden hatred
how do u expect me to go home
if u were my home?
(my road to heaven, darling)

there was no need to hurt me
you could have left without having to kill me
my love wasn't enough to keep u with me
and i don't know why
i didn't know what u wanted
so i gave u everything and u gave me
nothing back
            i want to forget the bad grace
but the pain won't let me
are we going out to paradise this friday?
the road is long
but i carry u in my arms like i carry your lies

look me in the eyes
tell me at least that u were mine
let me show u how i really loved u
how i truly loved u
          it's stupid
but u don't know what i would do
to see u by my side again
so come back to me

u can keep telling me lies
          u know i see the truth as one
god forgive me for forgiving u
but i don't wanna lose ya
it's painful to think that betrayal
never comes from our enemies
u were my best friend
(my favorite star)

we can still have a happy ending
u just have to shut your bad mouth
and stop pretending
love me, hate me
just be honest with me
          your love might have been little
but it was heavy enough to smash my eyes
(i was so blind, darling)

heaven is in your eyes and i wanna look at it

a tuberose in a rose garden

white tuberoses, red roses
i'm a writer
u know i won't cry but i will bleed
          my pain isn't just in my tears
it hides behind my lips
i hate having memory flashbacks
but it's nice when i remember
'cause i find they were the best ones
i've ever had

sometimes i pretend not to care when in reality
it's killing me like cancer
i waited patiently and desperately for healing
(it never came close to my heels)
i should have hugged u tight
the last moment i saw u
but the truth is
i didn't know u were thinking about leaving me
still u left me
and made me face the truth on my own
i shut myself away
          rotted like a tuberose

your promises were like candy
(u ate them and made more)
promises are the sweetest lies
u promised me u would stand by my side
until my eyes saw the angels
in the demons
          u weren't good for me
but baby, i deserved u
even though the stabbings
i remain say it was true love

big dreams, long illusions
u said i was important
and that there was no other like me
so i said:
like me there are many
            like u only presley's lies

what really hurts the most is knowing
we never said goodbye
and that u were just another dark poem of mine
i don't understand why u did that
if u loved me so much
sleeping has become impossible
since my mind connected the dots
            i cry every night
                my soul doesn't stop bleeding
u leave your monsters with me
now every time i try to fight
a piece of me dies
why was i but an option to u?
u were my priority
the way u left made me see the worst in myself

you hurt me, and baby, it's alright
i promised to love u and i won't break it
i still don't understand
why me?

        i guess i have to move on
                        move on
                        move on

but i have to seek out our lost love
one heart loved, one heart broken
          that's what i found in the end

we had so many plans, we were so happy
but then god took you away
          stole u out of my life
now, there is nothing left for me
i'm broken
my life is destroyed, my mind is ruined
(we never got it, did we?)

51

no woman leaves a rose garden
without blood on her hands

legendary star

u're the brightest star in my empty night sky
and the furthest away
your words are the cure that only time can heal
i could keep lying
but i don't wanna hear another goodbye
(not from u)
          please lord
i like to think that u and i are nikki in one
together we are mötley

promise me u'll remember this
when i'm gone again:
just because i don't show it
          doesn't mean i don't feel it
i adore u, my orange sky
(am i still your blue one?)
i can't lose ya
u know that if it happens
          i'll lose my senses too

the moon knows, and when she knows it
it's for certain
we haven't met by chance
u're the strength i need to clear my mind
          it hurts me to know
i haven't done half of what u did for me
but keep in mind
your love brought me heaven to earth
without having to die

don't leave me, seriously
i'm sorry i'm becoming a mess
things ain't easy
          i need ya
tell me at least
that i'll still mean something to u
when our moments become memories
          and your scars accessories
they are beautiful
and i choose not to know the story behind them

my life was complete when i saw people leaving
i have to admit that it killed me inside
i felt so empty as if i wasn't important
but then u showed up
made me feel talented and special
within the world
          i felt safe
i felt like i could tell u everything
but that changed as the months went by
i can no longer call you to save me
(i don't know why)
our lives seem to have changed overnight
i shouldn't have called your friend
          i shouldn't have done it
but i did it and there's no going back
i have already fallen without a voice to call

maybe you won't trust me ever again

i understand ya
maybe u won't adore me the same way ever again
maybe u won't wanna talk to me ever again
sometimes forever is finite, hon'
the future no longer finds us
            traveling the world

even after those other poems i wrote for u
your doubts still persist
if i'm going to watch you walk away
then let me make it simple for ya
u'll always remain in my memories
            u will be legendary
my favorite star, the brightest
the furthest
my legendary star

55

there may not be love between us
but there's a little light

mother

mother, i'm tired
if you'd hug me and kiss me
maybe i wouldn't have to cry myself to sleep
can't you feel the connection?
i haven't felt it in a long, long time

mother, look at me and tell me you love me
why do you only say that
when i'm falling apart?
do i only deserve your love when i'm sad?
why do you call me selfish?
i know i am
you didn't have to say it out loud
i know i'm stupid as hell
you didn't have to remind me

i love you
i love you so, so much
i'm sorry if i wasn't the ideal daughter
you don't know the shit that happened to me
i just can't tell you everything

i needed to find trust in someone else
'cause my heart was being crushed
by my inner hand
i found it, had my deepest secrets told
got left alone...
i believe that in our minds there's a glass cup
where the scariest secrets are stones
and others are paper
we pass the paper to someone else's cup
they can hold it
but if we pass the stone
            it starts to get too heavy

i have so many things i wanted to tell you
but they're gonna break your cup
you won't be able to handle it
          maybe, just maybe
if i told you... you would understand me
but i'd rather keep it to myself
than risk to destroy you
i still think about what would have changed
if i had told you
what happened that night... in our house
maybe we could get closer
          (the threat spoke louder)

thank you for the food you bought me
thank you for the clothes you bought me
but where are the goodnight kisses?
where is that "i love you" i heard so much
before i destroyed myself?

where is my mother?
          (my mom?)

just two more years...
just two more years until i get out of here
no matter what you do or say
i'm sure i'll leave home
thinking you didn't love me
and you'll be thinking i never loved you
          but i did
i just didn't show it
i was too worried about

                fixing
          m y s e l f

am i that hard to love?
so easy to hurt?

sweet lemonade

i know i can't say no
but do u really think i said yes to those two?
they took away from me
what should have stayed with me
            i was a fresh daisy
they pulled me out by the roots
and threw me back into the ground
as if i was nothing
like they hadn't in fact cut my throat

the threats were dangerous
their minds were a place of fear and terror
but what could i do?
i couldn't just tell everyone
they would think i was disgusting
even if i hadn't even asked for it

they messed with my mind in such a way
i didn't know if it was right
or wrong
their words made me understand
it was right, but now
now i think it was all a plan
to take away from me what would make me
sane today
            everything that is taken from us
is like a weapon for the future
it doesn't escape us, it makes us relive
that moment in a dark room
over and over again
whatever the things we choose or don't choose
to go through
changes the lines of our butterfly's wing
forever...

i'll keep drinking lemonade
until the acid kills me
          until it burns away
the memories of all those years
from all those malicious temptations
and unanswered touches

61

i was like a nabokov fresh daisy
and now i'm just looking forward
          to have my purity back

without you

i was with you
but you hurt me
i opened my eyes and saw your greed
but blinded myself again
i didn't wanna lose ya

when you left
i waited patiently for your return
when you begged me to stay
i asked god for a second chance
          my world went sparkling white
i tried to close my eyes
because of the brightness
and when i did
i saw nothing
there was nothing to be seen

as if a voice telling me
i couldn't live without you
that i would be nobody without you
but i am
          i'm a poetess
and my misfortunes are my art

i loved you
i loved you more than any other girl could
i stood up for you
and you took advantage of it

63

even after that madness n' sadness
i think i could still love you again
because truly i believe
that i never stopped loving you
          i still love you
the problem's not your rage
it's my vision
i saw beauty in your fury
saw love in your vices
saw myself in your blue eyes
everything bad u did to me
          i romanticized

god is the only one
who knows if i'm to lose you
but if that happens he can take me too

i would have won

i was loved by a boy
why didn't i stay with him?
because of my damn mind
          i could be in the middle of a fog
he would come after me
not knowing the rocks he would trip over
and the branches he would

              b   e
                  r   a   k

he tattooed my name on his heart
he tattooed my face on his eyes
            i was such an idiot
we humans actually know how to value a diamond
when it is lost

there wasn't a day that went by
that he didn't whisper sweet words
on my skin
i can admit that what i felt for him
          wasn't enough
on a scale, his love always fell down
i never knew how to appreciate it
and now i regret it
god... i regret it so much

if my new self had met him back then
we wouldn't have become strangers
i would have his songs, he would have my poems
we would be someone
            i would have won

---

he knew how beauty worked
not just physically but spiritually
even though i was but ordinary
          he saw me as an extraordinary girl
he always asked me about my books
he always waited for my "yes"
and when he stole that kiss from me
i should have held him longer
i should have kissed him harder

i know he won't read this
nevertheless i cry:
please
please...
i know you won't love me again
but i'm willing to seek your forgiveness
kiss your fingertips, lay my head on your lap

do you still write about me?
do you still wanna be mine?
do you still wanna have a future with me?
do you still wanna get high together?
do you still see me
within that other girl's eyes?
i see
i see you when some boy hurts me 'cause
i know you'd never do that
and i saw the chance to be a wanted
          and loved girl shattering
into a thousand bright spots in the sky

67

i lost you
and i lost myself too
i could have won you
          i could have won myself
i could have resisted
the temptations of my mind
but i gave up

3
love

red cigarettes

they're gonna kill me
          but i want one more
you're gonna hurt me
          but i want u

smoking red cigarettes
kiss me, your girlfriend doesn't care
love me until the night forgets us
(the stars know u were made for me)

baby, put on your leather jacket
'cause we're going for a ride
keep jesus in a pocket
          i'll pray for us on the wild (side)

romanticized cocaine on the dashboard
          (don't say anything to my lord)
u have been crowned my new king
your arms are my new string

give me another cigarette
can u stop, i'm not jealous
          i just wanna be yours
(give me one, give me two, give it up for me)

smoking red cigarettes
stay with me
i promise to love ya more than your babe
love me like the sun loves the rain
i know: at the rainbow's end there's u

breathing in red cigarettes smoke
it's like oxygen
when it comes out of your mouth
i love when it's u n' me and no one else
(don't blame me, it's my heart)

by your side the world seems dangerous
everything seems crazy
but i accept whatever you wanna do
'cause deep down i'm similar to u

take the rosary off my neck
we don't want the lord to see us sinning
he may even forgive ya
but i have already committed so many sins
just to see you in heaven with me

give me another red cigarette
u can keep hitting me, i'm not afraid
          u are everything an angel envies
(give me one, give me two, give it up for me)

be mine to burn
be mine to revive

eleanor bramble

dazzling margolis

i met her a year ago
not have much to say
just a few words

she is insecure
but gorgeous like an angel
she shines with her own heart
she doesn't need to steal anyone's shine
paradise is on earth
          no one has discovered it yet

even after an emotional fall
she gets up and makes everyone smile
the way her voice makes me want to hug her
until she actually breaks to a smile
          is unreal
she may not know what it's like
but she'll take the time to understand ya
(it's tiring)

the night is approaching, the day is fading
the liquor on her lips
makes her feel alive
she's not a rebel
she's just trying to enjoy life while she can

god, her skin's as brown as honey
eyes as dark as the abyss that took me
          to the world of wonders
she gave me a chance, fixed me
watched me fall apart due to human evil
          and fixed me again
with that dazzling margolis smile

if that girl keeps on the memories lane
          she will be here
i didn't give up, 'cause
she showed me the beauty
          and brilliance in life
(it's not as dark as i thought)
she also showed me kind people
u see...
kindness still exists
u just have to find it in the right places

i know she's afraid to do it
but i don't know why
people have already judged her
without even knowing her
          nothing else matters
besides her own happiness
there's no problem, darling
(there never was)

she doesn't know where to go
she doesn't know what to do
i'd better tell her:
          put on your best dress
             go out with your girls
have fun 'till the sun comes up
          u are alive!

don't give the world what it wants
it wants weakness
show that u are strong by being kind

listen to your music, wear what u want
            be what u want
the night is too short
to worry about tomorrow
            (people who know how to look
              know how to admire)

79

the world is a better place when i look
into your eyes

whiskey lover

i don't know if i've lived long enough
to write more poems
i don't want to repeat ideas
          i want to vary
but i can only tell about these people
and these subjects
(the same man)

he was older, yes
but i loved him, and oh...
i wanted so much to see that smile again
i swear to u
that man had the most beautiful of them all
          he gave me butterflies
every time he looked at me and smiled

so many poems i've written about him
it almost seems like a never-ending book
i want to show them to u
but it's too much
          poor thing
he little knows the feeling he created
in my heart
i believe that at first he must have thought
i was just another one
but baby
once loved, forever in my art

i told him:
my eyes melted when i first saw ya
and i may be boosting your ego
but it's just my mind talking
u said i was crazy, so
it's not like it bothers u that much
is it?

u were my type
(even though u weren't elvis)
u were a womanizer, a party animal
u loved to drink and talk to women
u loved the attention
            but not just mine
if u didn't care so much about the age gap
god only knows what u would be doing

            i love wild and crazy men
u were perfect for my inner woman
u liked submission, weed after midnight
and dirty promises

i changed so much after u sent me a message
over the days
whiskey became more of my lover than u
(i never thought i would lose u so soon)

even after the things u said to me
i continued and accepted your violence
but instead of staying
u chose to look for someone new
(can she love ya the same way i do?)

if u're hers, how can i be someone else's!?
i want u and only u
i will wait forever and ever!
            life is so unfair to those who love
i believed and still believe
u're my one true love
u are meant for me, u and me
my heart belongs to u!

82

i don't even know what i'm saying
but understand that i need u today
tomorrow, forever
so sad that my tears are nothing
          compared to your loneliness

every time u touched me my body trembled
look what u did to me!
i wanted u so bad
it was making me sick
baby, i was falling
and u didn't catch me
          now that i know u don't want me
how will i get back the love i gave ya?

don't say you love me when you kill me
and you bring me back

divine men tore

i know i'm not the girl you met the other day
          i know you wanted her back
but i can't just give her to you
you have to promise me
          you'll take care of her

i knew that same night
you'd be enchanted by the beauty
of my best friend
who wouldn't?
she's beautiful
but she would never, ever
love you the same way i do

i would make you shine like a diamond
i would do everything
to make your dreams come true
          i would do anything for you
              my fire
you don't need all these other girls
you need me

i know, believe me
i know she shines
(she's the most beautiful star)
          i shine too, but only by words
it's not enough

you say you're in love
i'm not that stupid
(i understand your hints)
so if you're really in love with someone
i pray to god that someone is me
            no one else
can make me feel so electric

i hope you still want me like you did before
(she can't take you away from me either)
            you were the only man
i ever truly fell in love with
please, please...
i beg you on my hands and knees
don't give up on me so easily
i love you too much to lose you now
stay where you belong
(lay in my heart and mind)

you must think you're smart
you chose the pretty friend
forgetting i know her like nobody else does
she won't romanticize your violence as i do
so stop playing around and listen to me
            you're divine!

do you understand my desperation!?
goddamn it
            i wanna be yours
i wanna be yours to breathe, forever
you're mine
even if you're not, you're mine

86

i can't compel you to love me back
(i know you won't)
but i'm gonna make you realize
          how much i want you
so please, if we're not meant to be
don't leave without saying goodbye

he didn't say goodbye

dead
you're dead
you're dead
and   u'r   dead
you can't
get out
of my
fucking
head

beautiful for ya

you said you would come
and i got all dressed up to welcome you
you said you didn't like the black
on my nails
so i painted them red again
            i'm waiting for you

in my black lace, with bare lips
and manicured nails
you always wanted a place in my heart
why can't i have it in yours?
i really want to be your girl
maybe it's a little hard for you
to understand 'cause
you're too busy going out at night
with those other girls

am i not pretty enough to be seen with you?
you're the only man i want people
            to see me with
to say - she's his and his alone -

choose me
no one ever chooses me
accept my new version, my excessive love
            my poetry
make me the girl worthy of your world
whisper to me, kiss me... come n' get me
i ask only this of you and if you do it
let me turn your skin to my writing sheet
your scent my favorite flavor
            your lips my starting point
                your hands my new clothes

what the fucking fuck is wrong with you?
tell me right away, i want to know
just don't say that the problem is me
i don't know what else i can be

you're the one who made me start this madness
repeated poems, repeated ideas
just for you to realize
            there is only you

give me something, i need to keep on writing
i can't stop here
i'm almost there, come like you promised
and maybe...
maybe there's more for me to write

the end

alphabetical index

about the author

eleanor bramble, better known as leonor silva, was born on december 21st, 2008 in viana do castelo, portugal. at just 15 years old and a visual arts student, she has already published a few poems in her school's newspaper and in a poetry anthology also published by her school.

with the publication of her first book, "the girl in black lace", eleanor bramble has started her career as a published poetess in 2024.

free poets collection

already published

Clarividência
(Vol. One)
Neusa

The Girl In Black Lace
(Vol. Two)
Eleanor Bramble

to be published

Maternidade
(...)
Luiz Machado

great authors collection

already published

1 - Um Pequeno Mal Por Um Grande Bem - Voltaire - Série Grandes Autores (I) - Tradução: Philipe Pharo | Fabiana Ribeiro

2 - O Gato Preto - Edgar Allan Poe - Série Grandes Autores (I) - Tradução: Philipe Pharo

3 - (não publicado)

4 - A Dama Com O Cão - Anton Tchékhov - Série Grandes Autores (IV) - Tradução: Philipe Pharo

5 - Os Idiotas - Joseph Conrad - Série Grandes Autores (V) - Tradução: Philipe Pharo

6 - A Alma Humana Sob o Socialismo - Oscar Wilde - Série Grandes Autores (VI) - Tradução: Philipe Pharo

7 - Em Terra de Cegos (O Bacilo Roubado e A Porta no Muro - H.G. Wells - Série Grandes Autores (VII) - Tradução: Philipe Pharo

8 - B.24 - Arthur Conan Doyle - Série Grandes Autores (VIII) - Tradução: Philipe Pharo

9 - O Sonho de Um Homem Ridículo - Fiódor Dostoiévski - Série Grandes Autores (IX) - Tradução: Philipe Pharo

10 - Os Mortos - James Joyce - Série Grande Autores (X) - Tradução: Philipe Pharo

11 - O Papel de Parede Amarelo - Charlotte Perkins Gilman - Série Grande Autores (XI) - Tradução: Philipe Pharo

12 - O Apelo Selvagem (The Call Of The Wild) - Jack London - Série Grande Autores (XII) - Tradução: Philipe Pharo

13 - O Escravo Heroico: Em Busca da Liberdade - Frederick Douglass - Série Grande Autores (XIII) - Tradução: Philipe Pharo

14 - A Mulher no Espelho (e outros contos) - Virginia Woolf - Série Grande Autores (XIV) - Tradução: Philipe Pharo

to be published

Manifesto do Partido Comunista - Karl Marx |Friedrich Engels - Série Grandes Autores (III) - Tradução: Philipe Pharo

other titles by contraatircse

already published

1 -   De Mim para o Mundo: Poesia e Fragmentos - Filipe F. Costa

1.1 -   Me and The World: Poetry and Fragments (Bilingual Edition Portuguese-English) (2nd Edition) - Philipe Pharo da Costa

1.2 - De Moi Vers Le Monde (Édition Bilingue Portugais-Français) (2ª Edition) - Philipe Pharo da Costa

2 - Poemas de Adil e um texto desalinhado - Filipe F. Costa (2ª Edição)

3 - Memoh Morto e 5 poemas de outubro - Filipe F. Costa (2ª Edição)

4 - Livro dos Poemas de Fruto Proibido do Doutor Armando do Sal e Outros Textos Neoexperimentais - Philipe Pharo da Costa (2ª Edição)

5 - As Meias do Poeta Victor Nuno de Menezes e Outros Fragmentos Físico-Teóricos - Philipe Pharo da Costa (1ª Edição)

6 - Este Aparelho Deve Ser Instalado Por Pessoas Competentes (Primeiro Manual) (1ª Edição\Capa Mole) - Philipe Pharo da Costa

6.1 - Este Aparelho Deve Ser Instalado Por Pessoas Competentes (Primeiro Manual) (1ª Edição\Capa Dura) - Philipe Pharo da Costa

7 - Contos Oblíquos - Philipe Pharo da Costa

8 - As Meias do Poeta Victor Nuno de Menezes (Po8 e Físico-Teórico) - Obra Completa - Philipe Pharo da Costa (1ª Edição/Capa Mole)

8.1 - As Meias do Poeta Victor Nuno de Menezes (Po8 e Físico-Teórico) - Obra Completa - Philipe Pharo da Costa (1ª Edição/Capa Dura)

to be published

Outras Mulheres - Philipe Pharo da Costa

A Fabricação da Luz - Philipe Pharo da Costa

x wonders of jack london
collection

already published

1 - Emil Gluck: O Pior Inimigo do Mundo; Vol. I (3ª Edição); Jack London; Tradução: Philipe Pharo da Costa

2 - Uma Invasão Sem Precedentes (Ou: A Guerra de Jacobus Laningdale); Vol. II (2ª Edição); Jack London; Tradução: Philipe Pharo da Costa

3 - O Conto das Mil Mortes - (Ou: O Navio da Tortura); Vol. III (2ª Edição); Jack London; Tradução: Philipe Pharo

4 - O Pagão; Vol. IV (2ª Edição); Jack London; Tradução: Philipe Pharo

5 - O Vermelho (Nascido-das-Estrelas); Vol. V; Jack London; Tradução: Philipe Pharo

6 - Cabeça Agachada; Vol. VI; Jack London; Tradução: Philipe Pharo

to be published

7 - O Silêncio Branco; Vol. VII; Jack London; Tradução: Philipe Pharo

brief note

with this book by eleanor bramble, *contra escrita* publishing gives continuity to its poetry collection "free poets" (poetas livres), started in portuguese, but in this case with an english written original that will be – hopefully – translated into portuguese.

this collection is part of the initial project of *contra escrita* in which its intended to give voice to poets and poetesses that are unknown to the general public.

www.ingramcontent.com/pod-product-compliance
Lightning Source LLC
Chambersburg PA
CBHW020728160726
47993CB00006B/2384